Watering my weeds
and
plucking my roses

Darrian Costin

Watering my weeds and plucking roses
First Edition Trade Book, 2022
Copyright © 2022 by Darrian Costin

Visit: Instagram: Darrian_costin_poetry

Editorial: Kerry wade, kerriganwade.com

This book is composed of several short poems and prose. Some of the poems may be triggering for some readers.

Please know that you are precious. You may feel alone, but you are never truly alone.

National Suicide Hotline:
800-273-8255

LGBTQ Suicide Hotline:
1-866-488-7386

Introduction

Dear dandelions,

Thank you. You are the reason; I have been able to do this. Watering my weeds and plucking my roses was written during a time in my life when I had undiagnosed trauma and PTSD. The only way I made it through that chapter of my life was through writing. The things I endured; the good, the bad, the ugly. All led me here. This book is a rollercoaster of emotions because I was a rollercoaster of emotions. I really hope you enjoy, the journey through the garden of my mind.

All the love,
Darrian

To my best friend and other half. Thank you for believing in me when I stopped believing in myself.

Contents

Unconscious

I've been trapped in my mind.

Suffocated by my thoughts.

Waiting for someone to notice,

*It's hard to see an **SOS** though,*

When it's painted on a smile.

Is it still heart breaking when your heart

is already broken?

I gave you every piece of me.

every cracked and broken piece.

only so you could brag about

"putting me back together."

My regret burns holes in my heart.

yours wishes it had a heart to burn.

My anger is telling me to tend to the sadness inside of me.

Tired.
a little sad.
Mostly tired though.

Sleep.
just to wake up,
tired again.

Food.
has no flavor.
Lost all meaning.

Showers.
haven't had one
in 5 days.

Communication.
Seems irrelevant
when you're on a sinking ship.

Help.
the hardest thing
I've ever had to do.

Days.
Aren't so dark.
Light in the tunnel.

   - Day by day

The humorous and sobering fact about life

is we all need love.

So much love,

we're willing to die for it.

Kill for it.

Even break our own hearts, if needed.

And so my tongue went numb with the abuse of having to hold it.

Impatient storms brew inside me.

The path of destruction whispers my name.

I remain unafraid.

*For I've danced with the **devil***

disguised as my lover

and dragged him all the

*way back to **hell**.*

My heart weeps for you.
I feel your hidden pain.
How the glow inside you
is starting to wane.

I woke up invisible this morning
made my way through the neighborhood.
Wasn't sure why or how it happened,
but the flowers under my bed were dead.

Don't flatter yourself, my dad broke my heart long before you.

The sad reality is I like it better alone
If you were to find me in a room
at a party all alone.
It was a choice.

Solitude is and always has been my comfort and best friend.

You are a rare one, they tell me.
"Your pain is worth your suffering,
every emotion brings you closer to the truth."

I am a **revealer** of lies and deceit.
A weapon among the weak,
talk freely, they know I am true.

They're drawn in,
entrusting me with everything.
Even things left **unsaid**.

In isolation I sob, SCREAM, ache.
Wading in another's emotional baggage
not knowing where theirs ends and mine begins.

Breathing through the pain
trying to **untangle** the mess
that is of both heart and mind.

Only to end up swallowing
the emotion, forever **hoping**
it doesn't affect me in the end.

  - Empath

The birds on the windowsill

Haven't moved a muscle

Not even the slightest of motion

Somehow, I know they're still alive

Waiting for the moment when they can finally die.

I sit in the dark.

Alone.

Wrapping myself

In the memories of what was.

   - Grievance

I thought my darkness made me weak, it makes me human.

Preconscious

It's so hard not knowing.
Not knowing if they care.
If they'll call.
If I pass through their mind at all.
Maybe they hardest part is the
if.

They see my magic and try to contain it.

Bottle it.

Keep it for themselves.

What they don't know is

my magic is unlike any other.

A consumption killer, if you will.

So I let them take it.

Bask in it.

Be on my way

& Watch them wilt.

> *- Energy vampires*

You are pure ecstasy.
Wait for no one.

The truth is a scary necessity.

It may shatter your whole world.

Leaving your heart bleeding in your hands

or have you speechless on a sunny day.

Feeling an internal glow that has long been missing.

You deserve to cry over spilled milk.

Caught in the middle of a never-ending
rainstorm trying to make shelter out of
a fragile ego and broken heart.

Asking why
I carried so much weight
on my shoulders.

No answer seemed to be good enough.
While I stood in the never-ending rain.
Staring at my hopes and dreams.

They haunt me.
Whispering my name.
Asking if I'll ever love myself enough

To do what needs
to be done to stop
this never-ending pain.

They tell me to calm down.

but

You can't bottle a hurricane.

They say eye contact is one of the most intimate things on the planet.

So why do we all avoid looking at each other?

"Do you see me?" She asked.

"Of course, I see you." I said

"But are you looking at me?" She questioned.

"Aren't those the same thing?" I asked puzzled.

"Seeing and looking are different. You may see thousands of things in a day, but when you look, you take the time to notice the beauty in each one."

- My reflection

It rained today,
marshmallow hearts
and emerald, green kisses.

They led me to a lake
of salty tears and forgotten wishes.
Where I thought of you.

You're like sugar coated medicine.

Artificially sweet with an awful aftertaste.

The air was fire.

My lungs were coal.

The space around me

was fighting me for control.

Whether immobile and frantic.

Or lost in the world of the unknown.

Just know you're a highly unwelcome guest.

- Panic attack

Make mistakes.

Live life.

People are unforgiving.

Regret is haunting.

A face of stone
protecting a soft interior.

- B*tch face

Muffled voices.
Pitch black darkness.
*You pulled the **shades** on my brain again.*

You're jerking my eyes
like a joke I'm
*the **punchline** to.*

I can hear them all
calling my name.
***Cold** cement on my face.*

Really have a way
of picking the worst place,
I have to hand it to you.

Finally coming to.
There's a crowd of people
and they're all here for YOU.

Now I have to
apologize
for your big show

Slow and steady,
that's what YOU decide.

Hard to move when
my stomach is like
a pile of rocks.

*My brain has turned to **mush**.*

A few days sleep.

I'll be fine...

You might be back.

No way to tell.

*The **unknown**, a feeling I know all too well.*

- Epilepsy

The love I so
desperately
seek is my own.

You're a giver.

Not a taker.

Sometimes it's too good to be true.

Always watering everybody else's plants.

Has me wondering,

When's the last time somebody watered you?

All my doors were locked.

So, I opened a window.

   - Baby steps

I heard this story once.

A man went around.

A collector of hearts.

Each woman gave it freely.

All unsuspecting.

Not knowing who he was.

None daring enough to accuse him.

Until half a century past.

A girl had asked,

"Why do you do what you do?"

Startled and scared,

he mumbled,

"I was born without a heart and theirs makes me feel

more human"

Don't let the essence of who they were
effect the progress of who you're becoming.

I keep it hidden under lock and chain.

So, no one around me can feel my pain.

Holding my pieces so close together.

Amazed at how I keep it all together.

I'll let you in on a secret my friend.

Even the whole are incredibly broken.

His tongue.
Agile and sharp.
Piercing yet hollow.

he spits venom with precision
and has the face of an angel.

She hid her heartache
deep within her bones.

Desperately trying to erase
the face that was etched into her soul.

Until she met you and remembered
that love wasn't always a game.

She then began to hold the heartache in her bones high on her
head like a crown.

The thing you're burying deep inside.
Could be the key to helping you thrive.

Do you feel the seeds planted in you?
Are you carefully tending to each one?

It's a beautiful thing,
to flourish.
See all the hard work you've done.

And in all her infinite wisdom she chose herself.

Let me go.

I can't.

It whispers, rattling my bones.

Why not?

What happens if you fall?

I'll get back up.

- Fear

Swallow me whole.

Chew me up and spit me out.

So, I can tell you.

You can't even chew properly.

Your branches thin and small.

Your trunk narrow and thin.

You worry your growing soon might come

To a slow and steady halt.

Worry not young one.

Plant near the water

and sow your roots unearthly deep.

Our sameness is what connects us.

To the reality that we are all here.

Not by choice,

by chance.

Our differences help us

see the changes needed for a better tomorrow.

If you think no one believes in you, you're wrong.

It may seem a little unbelievable, but
it's true.

I believe that you are making history for yourself.
No matter what anyone says.

I believe that you are stronger than your last rejection.
Get back up.

I believe that you will always know what's best for yourself.
Silence the voices.

I believe that you're right on time.
Water your seeds.

I believe in you.

Conscious

I catch glimpses of our future in that heavenly soaked smile.

Take a step inside.

Walk through the mucky waters.

Dig up the weeds that have been left unattended.

I should visit more often.

Give it my time and attention.

The garden will thrive and

The glow I harness is irreplaceable.

Just say it he says,

tell me about the imperfections that lie within you.

Show me the darkness that has been a long-kept secret.
Remove the mask and reveal your truth.

Your sin doesn't scare me, he says.
the deepest darkest parts of you are still worthy.

You live inside my head.

My favorite movie on repeat.

I felt you
before I knew you.
Don't ask me how,
but my soul just knew
it had found its missing half.

It's almost poetic
how my goosebumps
ache for your touch.

If people make you feel bad for being happy, then they're not your people.

Calm your heart.
Quiet your mind.
Can you hear it?
The healing of your own heart.
Be gentle with yourself.

She was a neatly pressed and
beautifully sealed envelope.

Full of untold secrets and messy memories.

Let the waves of security
wash over you.

Creating a blanket of comfort and stability.

Launching you into
your dreams.

Manifesting success, happiness, and serenity.

You asked me what I loved about you most.

Two weeks and I still need more time.

Time to gather all the words and emotions.

For,

How do you capture the essence of the wind?

You don't.

You bask in its quiet and sometimes wildly explosive moments.

Being grateful the wind is anything but boring.

It's bigger than you
and stronger than me.

The beautifully wicked thought.

Being at one.
Being free.

The days I'm with you compile into one.
One long hazy memory.

Spent undoing everything
the world has done to me.

Me and you
stuck on repeat.

An endless magical loop.
Where time stands still.

Pain is irrelevant
and healing becomes us.

Your voice was like a song.

One you were singing just for me.

Perfectly harmonized,

intoxicating my skin.

Seeping into my soul.

Traces of your lips still
dance on my hips
leaving me longing for
your bittersweet touch

Daydreaming of your face
and honey embrace
all of time slips by as I try
and remember why reality
is worth going back to

Only room for thoughts of you
as I lay my head on my pillow
impatiently waiting to fall asleep
because my dreams are finally
better than reality.

The lines in her face
were etched so deep
they themselves told a story.

Of importance, self-sacrifice, and infinite happiness.

If you're waiting for the perfect time.

The perfect day.

The perfect reason.

It will never come.

Perfect does not exist.

Please stop waiting.

Your time is now.

I used to be so carefree.
A whisper away from wild.

She's gone, shrunk inside me.
Hiding from the world.
Disguised as timid.

Waiting for someone to unleash the tempered beast.
Knowing that she can't be tamed and
probably never was.

The thunder echoed her anger.

It mirrored her rage.

Showing the world

Exactly how powerful she was.

Where the lavender grows dense
and the blackberry bushes are juicy.

Is a house with a little girl
who is over protected and
well directed.

With an ocean of fire in her heart.

Welcome me into

Your heart.

Your mind.

Your soul.

Summon me unto your body.

I've been patiently awaiting your call.

    - Consent

It's unfair.

The way you electrify every sensation in my body.

Without a single touch.

How just a glance

Leaves me breathless.

Urning for me.

So much more.

He was like math.

The kind with letters and numbers, difficult to solve, and never any help in my life.

She was like art.

Unrefined and messy, waiting to be appreciated.

Unzip me.

Reveal my inner workings.

Relish in the garden of my mind.

Experience indifference and tranquility.

Just don't forget to water the plants if you stay.

Part me
like the red sea.

Drench me
from head to toe.

Indulge me
in every inch of your sweetness.

Just please don't make me beg for more.

His silence surrounds me.

Screaming endless secrets.

In the best way possible.

- Infatuation

I tried to hide it.
Like the dark side of the moon.
Casting shadows over my love for you.

Until you exposed me.
Naked and bare.
My sins staring back at you.

You scooped me up
gently, all while
washing away the stains of yesterday.

Showing me that sin
is merely darkness
waiting for some kind light.

Your aura is intoxicatingly blissful.

Do the voices whisper to you in the dead of night?
Do they offer up the worst of advice?
Filling your head with doubt and fear
Telling you to just disappear.

Look around you, my love.
You are not alone.
Those voices you dread
Haunt everyone.

The voices will vanish
When they hear you say,
"I'm enough today and every day."

You're scary.

Scary like jumping off a cliff into ice cold water.

Scary like hiking to the top of a mountain.

Scary like free falling out of a plane.

Scary like believing in myself.

Scary like I never thought it would happen.

Scary like love.

We're connected
you and I

Our hearts
forever tethered
and cosmically aligned

We're bound
by souls and minds

No one
can undo
the magic in our bind

You're there.

When I close my eyes.
When I open them.

You're there.
Carelessly mocking me.
With that caramel skin
And those lust filled eyes.

I can feel the heat radiating off you from across the room.

Asking to devour me.
Begging me to give in.

- Foreplay

The way you make me laugh isn't a laugh at all.

*It's a **glow**.*

I wish I could read you like my favorite book.

Open you up and dissect you word by word.

Getting lost in the never-e   nding pages of your mind.

How I long to be invited on those pages.

My name written in that book.

As the one you call home.

Oh, how I wish I could read you like my favorite book.

We lay naked giggling
as our hearts dance
Hand in hand
rekindling the passion we share

   - Watering our garden

No words.

Just the rhythm of our hearts

beating in sync.

Tiny drums,

inside my ears.

Anxiously waiting,

for your solo

to fill my space.

Caressing every delicate piece of me.

Making sure I never forget the sound of

our song.

Printed in Great Britain
by Amazon

86436771R00057